Lektürehilfe: Mother to Mother

Für alle, die *Mother to Mother* im Englisch Leistungskurs als Pflichtlektüre für das Abitur lesen

Armin Ginkel

1. Auflage 2017

www.armin-ginkel.de

Gesetzt mit LaTeX in Computer Modern

ISBN: 978 1 5220 6064 2
Imprint: Independently published

Many thanks to Nicola Standley for proofreading and editing.

Contents

Workshops

The idea for this booklet came up during a workshop on exam preparation for the written Abitur exams in Hessen. You can find dates for workshops on Abitur exam preparation on *www.armin-ginkel.de*.

Disclaimer

The content of this booklet has been researched with great care. However, the possibility of errors cannot be fully excluded. Please send any remarks or corrections to *mail@armin-ginkel.de*.

Revision: 2b594f64

1 How to study a novel

- You will need to read the novel more than once. If you find the novel difficult, I suggest you first read the summary for each chapter before reading the actual novel. It makes sense to read once for gist and again for a closer examination of the plot, stylistic devices, etc.
- In order to keep track of the different aspects of the novel, I suggest you mark the text in different colours. Personally, I use three colours to mark different information in the text: I use green to mark the setting and basic elements of who is who in the novel. For example I mark the phrase "Lunga was born. Lungile, his father, ..." in green, because it tells me that Lungile is Lunga's father. Next, I use yellow for characterizations: I mark the sentence "The children do pretty much as they please" in yellow, as it characterizes the relationship between Mandisa and her children. Lastly, I use blue for stylistic devices and imagery in general. So I mark the phrase "Died like dogs" in blue, because it is a simile and dogs are a central motif in the novel.
- This helps you to concentrate on the narrative strategy: When you read, you want to exam-

ine how form (i.e. a particular choice of words, metaphor, etc.) has an effect on the reader.

- This booklet will give you some examples of important quotations and literary devices. However, you will have to find your own examples if you really want to demonstrate that you have a sound grasp of the novel.
- Keep track of the story. Keep a reading journal where you jot down notes on plot, characters, themes, etc. For each chapter, ask not only *what* happens, but also *when*, *how*, and *why*.
- For anything you want to say or write about the novel, provide evidence from the text. (You will find evidence more easily if you mark relevant passages and phrases as you read.)
- 'Mother to Mother' revolves around the history of South Africa. It is advisable to expand your knowledge of South African history and read up on individual events.

Story or Plot?

When we talk about the *story*, we refer to the events as they happen in a time sequence: First a white student takes her friends to Guguletu in her car. Then the car is stoned and the student killed. When we talk about *plot*, we talk about the causal relationships between events, i.e. *why* things happen. 'Mother to Mother' is very much concerned with *why* things happen: Mandisa wants to give us (and her "sister-mother") an idea of Mxolisi's world and wants us to understand *why* Mxolisi ends up being the person he has become.

---

2 Introduction: What literary genre is 'Mother to Mother'?

'Mother to Mother' is both an *epistolary* novel and a *historical* or *realistic* novel. Additionally, it is an example of *post-colonial literature*. Let us look at these terms in greater detail.

South Africa used to be a colony; it was part of the British Empire. We speak of *post-colonial* literature when we want to refer to literature that was written after the period of colonialism. More specifically, it is used to imply that a piece of literature deals with the effects that colonization and foreign rule have had on a particular society. In 'Mother to Mother', the narrator explains how colonialism, colonial settlements, and the resulting injustices during the apartheid regime had a detrimental effect on African societies. *Post-colonial* literature most typically presents history from the perspective of the colonized, which is also the case for 'Mother to Mother'.

The novel is also a *historical* novel in that it portrays the life of ordinary people in a realistic fashion. The novel contains and alludes to real historical events and the way these events exerted an influence on people. It does not mean that *all* of the characters in the novel actually existed in real life. Taking this into consideration, we have to ask whether or not the student who is murdered in the novel is in fact Amy Biehl; she is not referred to as "Amy Biehl" by Mandisa, the narrator. (This is also why this booklet does not refer to the victim as "Amy" - the novel is a work of fiction, so we must not assume that Mxolisi and his victim are meant to be the real-life murderer and victim.) The crux here is that the novel gives an idea of how the killer's world might have looked. This is what we mean when we say the novel is *realistic*: It is an attempt in fiction to describe how complex characters are influenced by social factors such as class, race, sex, prejudice, etc.

Finally, the novel is also an *epistolary* novel, which means it is narrated only through letters: In 'Mother to Mother', Mandisa, the killer's mother, writes a series of letters to the victim's mother. Thus, the narrative point of view is limited to that of a single character: We learn about the events only from Mandisa's perspective. This is plausible as one of the novel's aims is to describe the murderer's environment. Additionally, the purpose of writing the letters is to try and make the victim's mother understand and ease her pain, hence the need to address her directly. Furthermore, it makes sense in the context of *post-colonial* literature: It explains the world not from the colonizers' point of view, but rather from those who suffered as a result of colonization. Mandisa (re-)writes the history of South Africa from her perspective. With this in mind, the novel is not a justification of the murder, but rather an attempt at explaining the disparate worlds of Mxolisi and the young student he kills. The aim of post-colonial literature is to *decolonize the mind.*

3 An overview of the characters

Amy Biehl is the name of the student who was killed on August 25th, 1993. In the novel, her name is never mentioned except in the preface. It is unclear whether the white student in the novel is meant to represent Amy Biehl. (A novel, by definition, is fictional.)

China is Mxolisi's father. One day he disappears and never returns.

Dwadwa is Siziwe's father.

Funiwe is Mandisa's aunt. She first suspects that Mandisa's is pregnant when she stays with her grandmother.

Hlumelo is the name originally given to Mxolisi by Mandisa. (The name Mxolisi is given by China's clan.)

Khaya is Mandisa's brother. (see also: Nono)

Kukwana is Mandisa's mother (her girlhood name).

Lindiwe lives in the same street as Mandisa. She is one of Mandisa's neighbours who visit her to share her grief.

Lumka is one of the victim's friends. She tries to persuade the group not to go to Guguletu.

Lumko is one of Mxolisi's friends.

Lunga Lunga is Mandisa's second child. His father is Lungile.

Lungile is Lunga's father. He soon leaves to train as a freedom fighter.

Lwazi is "one of Mxolisi's staunch followers".

Makhulu is Mandisa's grand-mother. In order to avoid getting pregnant, Mandisa is sent to stay with her in a remote village.

Malume is Mandisa's uncle.

Mananga is a reverend who arranges a meeting between Mandisa and Mxolisi (when Mxolisi hides from the police).

Mandisa Mandisa is the narrator of the novel. She is Mxolisi's mother. She addresses the white student's mother directly. (The novel is an epistolary novel, i.e. a novel that consists of letters.)

Manono is Nono's mother (Manono lets Nono wear whatever she likes, including short skirts. Mandisa's mother does not approve.)

Mxolisi Mxolisi is the son of China and Mandisa. He is the white student's murderer. The novel revolves around Mxolisi's living conditions and why he commits murder.

Mzamo is one of two boys that Mxolisi plays with when he is a child. Both boys, Zazi and Mzamo, are killed by the police. This is traumatic for Mxolisi (cf. chapter 8).

Mrs Nelson is a white woman who Mandisa works for. (She is significant as a foil for Mandisa.)

Nobulumko is Khaya and Nono's daugher. Nobulumko means *Mother of Wisdom.*

Nohehake is the name given to Mandisa by China's family. Mandisa takes this as an insult. (cf. Chapter 8; *Hehake* is an exclamation with negative connotation.)

Nomabhelu is one of Mandisa's childhood friends in Blouvlei. Stella tells Mandisa that she has been married off to a man who is considerably older than her.

Nono is a friend of Mandisa's. Khaya, Mandisa's brother, and Nono are a couple. They have a child called Nobulumko.

Qwati is one of Mandisa's neighbours who visit her to share her grief. (cf. chapter 11)

Ribba is another of Mandisa's childhood friends. Ribba dies during an illegal backyard abortion.

Siziwe is the daughter of Mandisa and Dwadwa.

Skonana is one of Mandisa's neighbours. During the night of the police raid, she tells Mandisa that a white woman was murdered.

Stella is an old childhood friend of Mandisa's. When Mandisa goes on an errand for her mother, the two bump into each other. Stella tells Mandisa about Nomabhelu and Ribba.

Tatomkhulu is Mandisa's grandfather.

Yolisa lives in the same street as Mandisa. She is one of Mandisa's neighbours who visit her to share her grief.

Zazi is one of two boys that Mxolisi plays with when he is a child. Both boys, Zazi and Mzamo, are killed by the police. This is traumatic for Mxolisi (cf. chapter 8).

Character Map

(most important characters only)

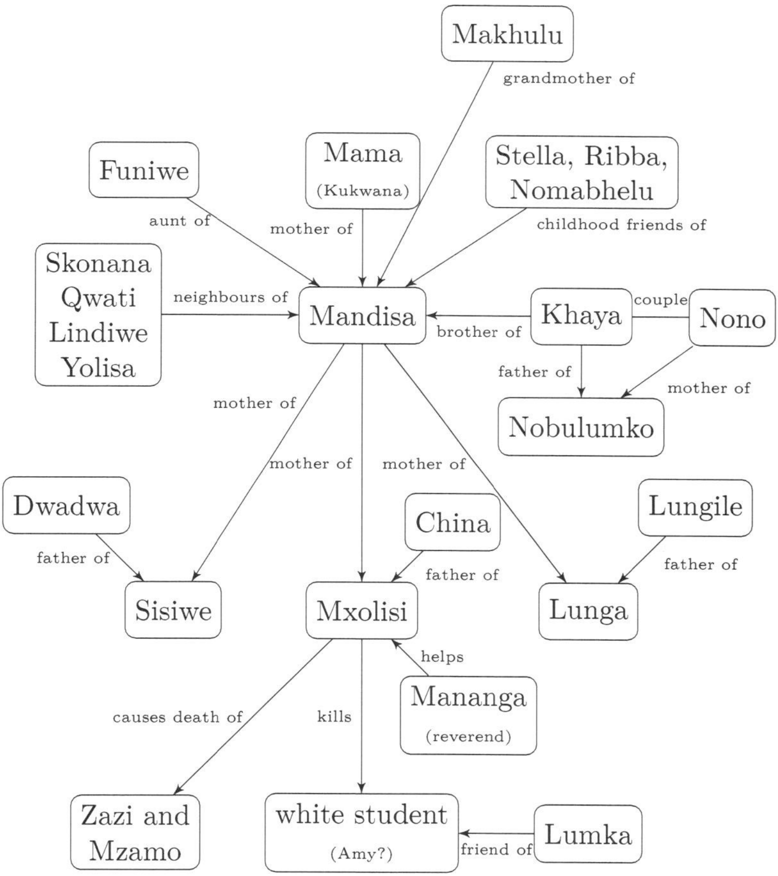

4 Chapter Overview

Chapter 1 - Mandisa's lament Mandisa introduces the main idea of the novel, shedding light on Mxolisi's world and her role as mother.

Chapter 2 - Mowbray - Wednesday 15 August 1993 Mandisa imagines the white student's life, which she assumes to be full of joy, while Mandisa's life is full of hard labour.

Chapter 3 - 5.15pm - Wednesday 25 August 1993 Mandisa compares her life to her white boss's. Also, she learns that somebody has been killed in Guguletu.

Chapter 4 - 7.30pm Mandisa gets home. Only Lunga and Siziwe are there, not Mxolisi. Mandisa learns that the person killed is a white woman.

Chapter 5 In a flashback, the reader learns about the forced removals when Mandisa was a child. Later in the chapter, we learn about Mxolisi's lack of education.

Chapter 6 - 4am - Thursday 26 August 1993 The police look for Mxolisi and search the house.

Chapter 7 In a flashback, Mandisa recalls the years 1971-73, when she is a teenager. She is sent away to live with her grandmother to avoid becoming pregnant. However, it turns out she has been pregnant all along.

Chapter 8 (Flashback continues) Mandisa marries China, Mxolisi's father, and moves in with his family. She is treated unfairly. China disappears, Mandisa leaves the household, meets Lungile and Lunga is born.

Chapter 9 - 6am - Thursday 26 August The police have finished searching the house and leave. Siziwe is in shock and Lunga badly hurt, beaten by the police.

Chapter 10 Mandisa reports how her grandfather told her about key events in South African history when she was a child.
Reverend Mananga helps Mandisa meet with her son, who is hiding from the police.

Chapter 11 Mandisa thinks about the murder and the guilt and shame that it entails. Her neighbours visit in a gesture of emotional support.

Chapter 12 Mandisa talks about the problems her son's generation has had to contend with. She describes the attack on the car and the murder.

5 Chapter by Chapter Summaries and Analyses

Author's Preface

Magona briefly discusses the murder of Amy Biehl, a white American Fulbright scholar who was murdered in Guguletu in August 1993. In Mother to Mother, the reader gains insight into the killer's mother's memories, and thus into the killer's world.

Chapter 1 Mandisa's lament

Summary

Mandisa, the killer's mother, addresses the victim's mother directly. She says that she had lost control over her son long ago and that the white student did not "belong" in a far-away township. She says that, on the one hand, the student did not realize how dangerous it was for her and, on the other hand, that she acted out of kind-heartedness. Finally, she closes by saying that now, in prison, her son has better accommodation and receives better food than at any time before in his life. She also points out that she, as a mother, has a heavy burden to carry, i.e. shame. (What she means is public disgrace.)

Important Quotations Explained

> Starting, if truth be known, from before he was conceived; when he, with total lack of consideration if not downright malice, seeded himself inside my womb.

This comment is ambiguous and can be understood in two different ways: On the one hand, it is clearly ironic. How can Mxolisi seed "himself" if he has not been conceived in the first place? On the other hand, Mandisa alludes to her feelings toward her baby. We learn about these feelings in detail as the novel unfolds: she holds her son responsible for all the missed opportunities in her life.
Also, Mandisa alludes to her impregnation without penetration. She thus employs religious imagery: The virgin Mary conceived Jesus without sexual intercourse. This is referred to as *immaculate conception*. Likewise, she evokes Shaka, a Zulu king, who is said to have been conceived during what began as a sexual foreplay.

> Did he not know they would surely crucify him for killing a white person?

Mxolisi, as her son, is seen as an insurgent who is punished, just like Jesus, who was *crucified* like a criminal. By using the verb *crucify*, Mandisa also implies that Mxolisi might be used to set an example, that he would be singled out from a larger group (cf. final chapter of the novel).

> Was she blind not to see there were no white people in this place?

Mandisa uses lots of rhetorical questions when she deals with the issue of how aware the white student is that she is in danger. Mandisa comes to the conclusion that the student's belief in her cause must have meant that she had "absolutely no sense of danger".

> White people live in their own areas and mind their own business - period. We live here, fight and kill each other. That is our business.

Mandisa appears to think of white and black people as a *binary opposition* (us and them); she does not think of South Africans as one people, but rather as a country divided by race. That's why she uses the pronouns "we" to refer to blacks as a distinct group.

Chapter 2 Mowbray - Wednesday 15 August 1993

Summary

Chapter 2 juxtaposes the student's world and the world of Guguletu. Mandisa contrasts the girl's comfortable life with her own deprivation. The reader gets to know the girl's and Mandisa's morning routine, the two women finally leaving their respective homes at exactly the same time. Mandisa is pressed for time: She works full-time and has to raise her children and perform her motherly duties. Mandisa introduces her children to the reader: her eldest son Mxolisi, his younger brother Lunga, and their sister Siziwe. Mxolisi and Lunga sleep in a tin shack in the backyard. Mandisa is tortured by the agonising knowledge that her children are not going to go to school that day, as teachers and students alike are on strike. The girl meets some student friends for lunch and decides to take them home (to Guguletu) in her car, a farewell gesture as the girl is about to leave South Africa. Her carefree life stands in stark contrast to Guguletu, where people suffer from tuberculosis. The chapter finishes by leaving the reader with the image of a "swarm" (of people) surrounding the car.

Important Quotations Explained

> Your daughter has been a very good friend, full of enthusiasm and eager to learn: [....] Not a trace of arrogance in her ... so full of childlike zest.

Mandisa underlines the girl's kind-heartedness, although it is hard to say whether or not her account is ironic. The phrase "full of childlike zest" might imply that her ideas are unrealistic and that she does not comprehend the problems blacks have to contend with. (*Zest* means enjoyment and enthusiasm.)

> They have no idea how hard life is; and if they're not careful, they'll end up in the kitchens and gardens of white homes ... just like us, their mothers and fathers.

In the novel, not only does Mandisa draw a line between blacks and whites, she also thinks of parents and their children as inherently different when it comes to how each group experiences life in South Africa. Mandisa says the younger generation has "no idea" about life.

> 'I insist! You cannot refuse me this last wish', your daughter jokes.

In this case, "last wish" is ironic (see *dramatic irony* in the list of literary devices), as it refers both to the student's final days in South Africa and also to the last thing she does before she is murdered. In the previous paragraph, Lumka, one of her black friends feels "uneasy" and is "adamant" that she should give them a ride, but the others do not agree and Lumka falls silent. This is one of many cases of *foreshadowing* in the novel.

Chapter 3 5.15pm - Wednesday 25 August 1993

Summary

Mandisa compares her life to that of the woman she works for, Mrs Nelson. While Mandisa has no free time, Mrs Nelson has enough time to go to the gym, meet up with her best friend, Miss Joan, to enjoy breakfast with her friends, go shopping, visit fancy restaurants etc. (Mrs Nelson is afraid that she might get fat, though.) In the novel, she is a foil for Mandisa: When you compare the two women's lives, Mandisa's sorrows become more obvious. On this particular day, Mrs Nelson comes home early from her "day off" and tells Mandisa to quickly go back to Guguletu as there seems to be trouble there. She insists on Mandisa leaving and even gives her a ride to the station. On her ride home, Mandisa and the other passengers speculate about what is happening. Mandisa compares the situation in Guguletu with that in Blouvlei. People were forced to move to Guguletu and leave Blouvlei as the government wanted residential areas to be segregated. At the same time, the government underestimated the number of homes that would be needed, causing a housing shortage in the new place, Guguletu. Also, there weren't enough schools. Mandisa points out that life expectancy has actually been decreasing since they had to move to Guguletu. Mandisa describes the atmosphere in Blouvlei just before the mass removals: it was characterized by rumours and, later on, by disbelief. Rumour has it that a car has been stoned and set fire to. Mandisa is even more anxious than before, hoping that Siziwe is at home with her brothers to protect her. Getting home, she sees Siziwe at the door. At this point in the novel, neither Mandisa nor the reader know whether Mxolisi or Lunga are at home.

Important Quotations Explained

> She [Mandisa's employer] never takes me to Guguletu. White people are not allowed to go there. We reach the bus terminus near the station and find pandemonium king.

The word *pandemonium* means *chaos* and is repeated several times throughout the chapter. It is used both to describe Guguletu after the murder that the book deals with, and to describe Guguletu in 1968, when Mandisa's family is forced to leave Blouvlei and move to Guguletu. It is used to characterize the individual's life as well as the township as a whole (see also chapter 4 for "pandemonium" to describe the situation in Guguletu).
Another aspect that is striking in this quote is that Mandisa says white people are "not allowed" to enter Guguletu. The phrase "not allowed" sounds like this is a law, or at least a widely-agreed tacit agreement. Thus, the young student's decision to give her friends a ride is called into question.

> Good things are scarce in Guguletu. [....] There is no harder luck for a dog than to be a stray in a place of poor people. What is such a dog to benefit, when the people themselves gnaw and chew bones to powder, suck in the last bit of juice therefrom before spitting out the useless pulpy matter.

Mandisa elaborates on scarcity in Guguletu. She ponders the fate of dogs in a poor neighbourhood: Basically, what Mandisa says here is that humans themselves are like dogs in Guguletu. They live like animals and search the rubbish for food. Humans, in 'Mother to Mother', are frequently compared to dogs (and animals in general). The dehumanization of individuals and human beings in general is one of the central themes in the novel. It is to come up again later in the novel (cf., for example, the fate of Zazi and Mzamo in chapter 8).

> Our inability to imagine certain forms of evil, the scope and depth of some strains of ruthlessness.

With regard to the forced removals, Mandisa contemplates the nature of evil, coming to the conclusion that people are unable to imagine "certain forms of evil". In conceding this, Mandisa puts her judgement of the murdered student into perspective: the student has not been able to imagine what might happen to her in Guguletu, just like people had not been able to imagine the government forcing them to leave their homes.

> Unless, of course, it is a grandchild whose arrival is an abomination - the children our children are getting before we even suspect they have come of child-bearing age.

In this chapter, Mandisa states that illegitimate children are an "abomination" (something that is disgusting and outrageous), adding the adverbial "of course", as if this is taken for granted. As it turns out in the novel, Mandisa herself is merely a teenager when her first child is born. Additionally, we learn that public disgrace plays a pivotal role in South African society.

> Instead of easing my anxiety, the answer plunged me deeper into the hell of uncertainty.

What is agonizing for Mandisa is the "hell of uncertainty": she does not know if her children are safe. She does not realize that it is not her daughter she has to worry about - another example of *dramatic irony* in the novel.

Chapter 4 7:30pm

Summary

Siziwe tells Mandisa that Lunga is home, but that Mxolisi is not. Siziwe does not seem to be bothered by this. Mandisa briefly thinks about the relationship of "womb siblings"

7:45pm

Their neighbour Skonana bangs on the door. She informs Mandisa that a white woman was killed in their part of Guguletu, close to where they live. Skonana says the woman has been stabbed with a knife (not necklaced, like Mandisa feared).

Important Quotations Explained

> Lunga was either asleep or reading a book. The house could burn down before that one noticed the fire, his eyes were forever buried in something he was reading.

It is striking that Lunga is inherently different from his brother. Generally speaking, outside forces and conditions are similar for Lunga and Mxolisi. Mandisa hints at the question of whether we are shaped solelyby our surroundings only. The question might boil down to the following: Can we choose freely or are we fated to certain actions by the environment we are in? (The relationship between the individual and society, and also between free will and determinism, is one of the key questions discussed in sociology and social philosophy.)

> Guns are as common as marbles were when we were growing up.

In this comparison, Mandisa makes it clear that conditions for are dramatically different compared with conditions when she was young. (See chapter 5 for a description of her childhood.) In her comparison, Mandisa effectively says that guns are omni-present and that they are the toys of today's children.

> We know that many innocent people have died in their [the police's] hands. Their blood-stained hands. Died. Killed by the police. With impunity they killed our people in the past.

Mandisa explains that the police are despised and feared in Guguletu. They cannot be trusted and have often treated people badly. While the police can kill people without punishment ("with impunity"), the killing of a white woman, Mandisa is sure, will spark a lot of police violence in Guguletu. Mandisa goes on to explain that killing a white woman was "quite another thing".

Chapter 5

Summary

Skonana, Mandisa's neighbour, asks her to come over to her place. Mandisa declines, feeling weak and tired. Mandisa says she wants to lie down. What follows is a prolonged flashback dealing with the forced removals of Africans when Mandisa was a child.

At nine years of age, Mandisa spends a generally happy childhood in Blouvlei. Her mother only works part-time and has enough time to look after Mandisa and her brother Khaya. Mandisa is allowed to play outside until sunset. The family has an intact social network.
Initially, rumours about an impending removal are dismissed as unrealistic. Her brother Khaya tells Mandisa that

Tat'uNonjayikhali, a most unreliable person, started the rumour, which slowly subsides.
This changes drastically when one day a plane appears in the sky. The children are frightened when the plane emits a cloud of what turns out to be paper.
People are shocked when they realize that these papers announce the removal of all residents of Blouvlei to Nyanga. Numerous meetings are held; the government refuses to speak to a delegation. The community manages to postpone the date of the removal to September, but ultimately all attempts at calling off the removal fail.
In the early morning of September 1st, the demolition of houses begins and people are forced to leave. A lot of residents get injured during the removal, desperately trying to take with them whatever they can (such as used building material).
The ensuing trek takes people through the enormous farms and land of whites. In Guguletu, their new home, conditions are not as favourable as they were in Blouvlei: Women have to work full time as their husbands wages are low. Generally, people are stressed and dissatisfied.

Important Quotations Explained

> Who would come to this accursed, God-forsaken place? This is what I want to know - what I can't begin to comprehend. [....] What was she doing there, your daughter? [....] Not an army of elephants would drag me here, if I were her.

Before Mandisa goes on to explain living conditions in Blouvlei, her childhood home, she employs a couple of rhetorical questions to express doubts regarding the white student's decision to come to Guguletu. In her comparison, Mandisa makes it clear that while the student decided to go to Guguletu of her own free will, Mandisa and her family are forced to live there - against their will.

> An extra one she did not put with the others in the brown bag but handed directly to me.

Mama Mandila, who sells *vetkoek*, a traditional South African fried bred, does not only give Mandisa the ten vetkoekies she is supposed to buy on an errand for her mother, she also hands Mandisa an extra one just for herself. This represents the idea that in Blouvlei good things happen to Mandisa: people are kind-hearted and there is enough of everything to enjoy life.

> All? To the last one? Our parents laughed. Obviously, the government didn't know what it was talking about. [....] In similar scenarios or variations thereof, one thing all had in common, was people refuting the unpalatable.

As Mandisa briefly mentions in chapter 3, people are unable to imagine the government committing a crime of this unprecedented magnitude. The thought is so terrible that people resort to denying the possible validity of the rumours. This is another example of dramatic irony in the novel: The reader, just like the narrator, knows that the rumours are true, while people find them absurd.

> Then one day, the rumour, all grown and bearded, armed with the stamp of the government, returned.

Here, the impact of the people realizing the truth of the rumours is even underlined by means of personification: the rumour itself is "grown" and "bearded" (like a child that has grown up to be a man).

> Khaya, because he was a boy, didn't suffer from restrictions as I did.

This quote refers to her mother calling Mandisa home in

the evenings. It marks a slight criticism of life in Blouvlei as Mandisa is treated differently from her brother, simply because she is a girl. This foreshadows the way Mandisa is treated as the novel unfolds, particularly when she gets pregnant and in dealings with China's family.

> On this day, however, the manner of its [the plane's] appearance, so close to the ground, so close to us, put this wonder on the same level as the burning bush, the water-sprouting rock and talking serpents of the Bible.

Mandisa compares the plane to different stories in the Bible: Firstly, God made himself known to Moses thorugh the *burning bush* when he commanded him to lead the people of Isreal out of Egypt to Canaan, the promised land (cf. Exodus 3:1-17). Secondly, God makes water come out of a rock for the people of Israel on their way out of Egypt (Exodus 17:1-7). Ironically, in the bible Moses leads people from Egypt, away from slavery, to Canaan, the promised land God himself had designated for his chosen people. In South Africa it is the government that "designates" land to the Africans. The plane thus announces the end of paradise (i.e. Blouvlei), the exact opposite of the two biblical stories mentioned.
This ties in with the third reference Mandisa makes, the talking serpents of the Bible: In the bible, serpents often represent the devil, who is cunning and deceptive. He talks Eve into eating the apple from the tree of knowledge and thus makes God expel both Adam and Eve from paradise.

> In a cloud of pink-fleshed faces peeping from beneath heavy helmets, [...] the white men set upon the tin shacks like unruly children destroying a colony of anthills.

Here is another example in which Mandisa metaphorically describes human beings as animals: The black population of Blouvlei are portrayed as ants which are destroyed by "unruly children" (whites). This can be seen as a euphemism:

Mandisa makes it clear that in the eyes of the whites, blacks are merely insects; it does not matter whether or not they are "destroyed". (Three paragraphs down, though, the attack is labelled "pitiless" and "ruthless".)

10.05pm - Wednesday 25 August 1993

Summary

Mandisa ponders the fact that Mxolisi is different from the other children in that he is disobedient. Dwadwa (Siziwe's father) returns from work and brings along some meat. They have dinner. Mandisa explains to the reader that violence as such is nothing out of the ordinary, but the victim being white is. She tells the reader an anecdote of what happened in the 1960s: Assuming their presence as witnesses would prevent police violence, three nurses from Belgium went to South Africa. They were, however, "beaten up" by blacks, had to be hospitalized, and then left the country as fast as they could.

Mandisa points out that Mxolisi, while being 20 years old, is still in Standard 6 at school, i.e. a level intended for twelve- to thirteen-year-olds.

Mandisa adresses the student's mother directly again ("and your daughter"), asking whether she did not feel a "natural sense of unease" when entering Guguletu.

Mandisa and Dwadwa talk before going to bed. Mandisa sheds light on how bad the school system has always been for blacks in South Africa. And, if anything, the situation has only deteriorated in recent years. She then goes on to explain how violence began to spread: It was first directed against whites and their property. It then extended to black people's homes and cars, until finally, a black person was stoned and subsequently "necklaced" to death by a black crowd. Mandisa states that the brutal way of killing people by "necklacing" has only been done to blacks, not the "oppressors". (*To necklace* means to murder somebody by forcing a burning tyre around their neck and arms.)

Important Quotations Explained

> But I know that we, parents, have become toothless dogs whose bark no one heeds.

Mandisa states that parents do not have any power over their children any more. The children do not listen to ("heed") whatever they say ("bark").

> Whites are dogs!

Mandisa concedes that it is her generation who told their children that "whites are dogs". The word *dogs* is, of course, negatively connoted here. The metaphor of dogs (and animals generally) can be seen to go hand in hand with what Mandisa calls "clothing satanic deeds with innocent apparel" when she talks about the term "necklacing": The dehumanization of the people of Africa, both black and white, is reflected in their being referred to as animals. Just like the term "necklacing", it constitutes a euphemism, making the actual brutality of the deeds appear less tragic.

Chapter 6 4am - Thursday 26 August 1993

Summary

Mandisa and Dwadwa are in their bedroom. Dwadwa is fast asleep, but Mandisa is not. She is too worried. The silence of the night is broken by the sound of a car door closing. Mandisa fears that Mxolisi has hijacked a car. It soon turns out, however, that the house has been surronded by a large group of people. Siziwe comes running into her parents bedroom; she is terrified. Mandisa is not sure whether it is the police or a group of common criminals. She cannot say which would be worse.

When Dwadwa opens the door, he is injured as the police storm into the house. Mandisa and Siziwe panic. The police demand to know the whereabouts of Mxolisi. When Mandisa says she does not know, she is hit by one of the police officers. In the ensuing search, the police destroy the *hokkie* (the garden shed) and cause damage throughout in the house. Finally, the police viciously beat up Lunga. They say that as Mxolisi's brother, he should know exactly where Mxolisi is.

Important Quotations Explained

> I blew the candle out and watched the dying glow of the taper.

A candle signifies light in the darkness of the individual's life. It also implies illumination. Note how Mandisa relights the candle later in the chapter, and how the light is then extinguished once again when the police enter the house. Light also means life, while darkness means death. The dying glow of the taper could be interpreted to imply that Mandisa's hope is slowly but surely dying as a result of the uncertainty revolving around Mxolisi.

> Not at all a bad boy. Just a young person taken up with this business of politics. As all the students have been these past twenty years or so. Why, only two weeks ago, did he not risk his life saving a girl from a group of men who wanted to rape her?

Just like in the previous chapter ("All children are like that these days."), Mandisa asserts that Mxolisi is in many respects not different from his peers at all. Additionally, she wants to say that his generation is a victim of circumstances and prejudices. The picture that Mandisa paints of Mxolisi is ambiguous: On the one hand, he is disobedient and Mandisa is worried he might have hijacked a car. On the other hand, however, she says he is "not at all a bad boy", having saved a girl from being raped by a group of men. Mandisa wants the reader to accept this ambiguity as she presupposed Mxolisi is as such inherently good, but led astray by the appalling conditions of life in a township in general.

> And at times it is hard to know which is worse.

Mandisa does not know yet, whether it is the police or a group of criminals who have surrounded the house. It is ironic that, for Mandisa, both options are equally terrifying: The police represent the law and the authority of the state in general. However, this very authority is what people in Guguletu fear. Furthermore, Mandisa thinks about the possibility of being murdered, be it by the police or criminals.

Chapter 7

Summary

Again, Mandisa addresses the student's mother directly, stating that Mxolisi has consistently meant trouble for her since the day he was conceived. This takes the reader on a flashback to the years 1971-1973: From the parents' generation's view, education should enable the children's generation to gain access to a better life (compared with their parents). Pregnancy, however, would stand in the way: In February 1971, when Mandisa is not even fourteen, puberty hits and her life changes drastically as her mother is worried she

might get pregnant. Things get worse when Khaya, Mandisa's brother, makes Nono, a friend of Mandisa's, pregnant. Mandisa learns that an illegitimate pregnancy means public disgrace. When she goes on an errand for her mother, she meets Stella, an old childhood friend. Stella tells her that several former schoolmates got pregnant. As the chapter unfolds, it turns out that one of Mandisa's schoolmates has actually died during an illegal *back-yard abortion.*
Her mother grows increasingly worried and insists on *inspecting* Mandisa to make sure she is still a virgin. Mandisa and China, her new boyfriend, meet in secret. China understands they cannot have sex, so they have *play sex* (without penetration).
When Mandisa learns that Nono is pregnant, she is mad: She says it is the girls responsibility to prevent pregnancy. She criticizes the way Nono dresses (short skirts, etc). Tensions between Mandisa and her mother intensify until, finally, her mother decides to send Mandisa to Gungulutu, a village where Mandisa's grandmother, Makhulu, lives. It is a remote place in which Mandisa's mother spent her childhood years. Mandisa detests having to go to Gungulutu and being separated from China.

Important quotations explained

> Not after that first unbelievable shock, his implanting himself inside me; unreasonably and totally destroying the me I was. The me I would have become.

Mandisa is here referring to her perception of the pregnancy and how it affects her life. Interestingly, it is Mxolisi, not China, who *plants* himself inside her. "Destroying the me I was" implies that on the one hand, this is a violation of her body, an act of violence committed by her son, who has not been born yet. On the other hand, "the me I was" and "the me I would have become" refers to how Mandisa's life would have unfolded if it hadn't been for the pregnancy. Her very identity is changed through the pregnancy (and quite literally so, as you are going to see later on).

> Nomabhelu, another ex-Blouvlei girl, had been married off to a man old enough to be her father, Stella said.

In many respects, this sentence is telling when we look at the role of women in South-African society. Nomabhelu is not allowed to make decisions for herself, not even when they are as pivotal as choosing a husband. This is underscored through the use of the passive voice ("had been married off"). The phrase "another ex-Blouvlei girl" implies that this was common practice in 1970s South Africa and that Nomabhelu is just one out of many.

> 'And the less you or Khaya see of that she-dog, the better,' she said. 'I don't like her ... and never will.'

Here, Mandisa talks about Nono, who goes to school with Mandisa and Khaya. Also, she has been Khaya's boyfriend and is now pregnant. This scene makes it obvious how furious Mandisa's mother gets at the thought of an illegitimate, teenage pregnancy. The term *she-dog* implies that Mandisa is like a female dog who would have sex with anybody. Interestingly, she accuses Nono and the way she dresses and makes her alone responsible for the pregnancy, see further down: "It is the girl's responsibility".

> Fourteen, almost. Banished to a far-away desert.

Note that this passage can be interpreted as an allusion or reference to 'Romeo and Juliet'. In the play, Juliet, like Mandisa, is just under fourteen. In 'Mother to Mother' it is Mandisa who is banished, while in 'Romeo and Juliet' Romeo is banished after killing Tybalt. Note that the word *banished* is re-iterated over and over again in this chapter; it is the same word used in Shakespeare. (You also might want to consider investigating how Mxolisi could be compared to Romeo.)

Gungulutu - September 1972

Summary

It is just before dawn. Mandisa is lying awake. It is the last day of school before the holidays. Mandisa has been staying in Gungulutu, her mother's childhood home, for three months now. Mandisa acknowledges her grandmother's efforts in making her feel comfortable, cooking her favourite meals etc. This, however, does not mean Mandisa is not pensive about the relationship between her and her mother.

Three weeks before the end of the school year, they receive a letter from Aunt Funiwe, who Mandisa has never met. The letter says that Aunt Funiwe is expecting a child and that she is going to visit Gungulutu to give birth to her child there. Makhulu, who is illiterate, makes Mandisa read the letter to her over and over again. They talk about the possibility of Mandisa staying at Aunt Funiwe's in East London to attend secondary school there and to help Aunt Funiwe with her child.
Mandisa immediately sends a letter to China telling him to apply to schools in her aunt's area so that they could see each other when Mandisa starts high school.

On the last day of school, children are allowed not to wear their school uniforms. They clean up the classrooms and then assemble to receive the results of their end-of-term test. Mandisa comes second best in her class (out of 33). She is very proud as she is sure China would be proud of her, too. On her way back from school, she collects a letter from China from the village shop.

Mandisa's aunt arrives. As she looks at Mandisa, she suspects that Mandisa is pregnant. Only then does Mandisa realize that she has not had her period during her entire time in Gungulutu. The village midwife examines her and comes to the conclusion that Mandisa is pregnant and, at the same time, still a virgin.

Malume, Mandisa's uncle, sends a telegram to Mandisa's mother, who comes to the village by car. After receiving the news, she is worried about what people in her church will think of her family. Aunt Funiwe insists that Mandisa has brought no shame on the family, calling the pregnancy an "accident" (p.113 l. 21). Likewise, she insists that the family's prime concern should now be to support Mandisa and her baby.

Mandisa is concerned, because her mother does not make it clear that, in her eyes, Mandisa is innocent. Mandisa feels hopeless; she does not know what to do.

Important quotations explained

> I lay wide-eyed staring at the ceiling ... Now, wide-eyed, I lay on the bed, blankets flung to my feet, eyes wide with excitement.

When faced with uncertainty, Mandisa is sleepless. The former of the quotes simply refers to the fact that Mandisa's mind is in Cape Town with her boyfriend China. It refers to one out of many sleepless nights Mandisa experiences in Gungulutu. The second quote, however, while also dealing with Mandisa's uncertainty, is actually about her excitement at the thought of moving to East London together with China. Mandisa cannot wait to hear what China thinks about her plan. (When it comes to sleeplessness, cf. also the beginning of chapter 6, when the police raid is impending.)

> But of late, God had been less than inattentive to my prayers; [...] I thought it best not to depend on Him wholly.

Mandisa does not depend on her prayers and on God alone. For several reasons, the word *wholly* can be seen as a pun: Firstly, later in the chapter, the word *whole* is referred to describe Mandisa being a virgin when she arrives in Gungulutu. Thus, depending on God *wholly* could mean a virgin depending on him. Secondly, *wholly*, *holy*, and *holey* are homophones. Thirdly, in saying that God has not answered her prayers, saying that she does not depend on them *wholly* now, is an understatement.

> With time, you know that if you have kneaded, the dough will certainly rise. I knew that, sooner, or later, therefore, everything would become clear ... obvious.

What Makhulu means is that if Mandisa is pregnant, she would see this from her belly sooner or later. (When Mandisa and her mother arrive in Gungulutu, Makhulu is assured that Mandisa is "whole".) She cannot think of any other way to ascertain whether or not Mandisa is pregnant. At the same time, she does not feel the need to, as Mandisa has been behaving herself exceptionally well during her stay. Thus, Makhulu compares the foetus with a cake that rises in the oven. Likewise, she compares sexual intercourse with kneading the dough before it goes into the oven.

> Auntie Funiwe. So much store had I put on her coming. Made great plans, banking on her benevolence. But, the very next morning following her arrival, not only did those grand plans unravel but my very life came to an abrupt halt.

This statement, taken from the final paragraph of the chapter, aptly shows the situational irony involving Aunt Funiwe: From the point of hearing the news of her aunt's pregnancy,

Mandisa hopes that her aunt will finally bring about the *salvation* that Mandisa is yearning for. In the end, her arrival precipitates disaster. Additionally, when comparing the two pregnancies, ironically, her aunt's pregnancy means joy and hope, while Mandisa's pregnancy entails "Fear. Shame. Anger." Again, light, i.e. the following morning, means that the truth comes to light. Note that contrary to what readers might expect, light here is not to be confused with hope. Ratherm it shatters hope as the full extent of the calamity becomes clear.

Chapter 8

Summary

Chapter 8 also opens with a direct address to the student's mother. Mandisa laments the ignominy, i.e. public shame, that her son's deed entails.

Chapter 8 continues the flashback from the previous chapter. It deals with Mandisa and her mother's ride home. Their driver, a quiet man, starts on a rant when they drive through a farm that extends over a very large piece of land. Their driver finds it remarkable that a single white farmer owns hundreds of cows. He asserts the land was stolen. In Cape Town, the situation for Mandisa is even worse compared with Gungulutu: Her mother does not allow her to leave the house at all. Instead her mother watches her all the time, even taking time off work.
Meanwhile, Nono has had her baby. The baby's name is Nobulumko (Mother of Wisdom).

Mandisa and her mother disagree on whether or not China should know about the pregnancy. Finally, Mandisa manages to sneak a letter to China - the neighbour's twin daughters help her. When China eventually shows up, Mandisa does not anticipate his reaction: China cannot accept that Mandisa is expecting his child. He says he is planning to go to boarding school and that he has been granted a scholarship. The meet-up does not go well. Mandisa tells China not to enter the house again, ever.

Mandisa's unlces take her to China's family to negotiate the situation. They again affirm Mandisa's virginity. China's family agrees to think about the issue and come to a decision at a later point in time.

Two months later, a white priest makes it clear to China that it is his duty to marry Mandisa. The baby is born on January the fourth, 1973. Mandisa has ambiguous feelings about the baby, but finally feels joy about the baby that she names *Hlumelo*. Her father supports Mandisa in her wish to continue her education. Also, Mandisa and he agree that it might not be the best decision to marry China. However, final decisions cannot be made by either Mandisa or her father. Rather, it is the clan that decides. Thus, Mandisa and China finally get married.

As custom dictates, Mandisa moves in with her husband's family, who give Mandisa her name of wifehood: They call her *Nohehake*, which Mandisa takes as an insult but nonetheless feels she has to accept the name. China's family is amazed to hear that Mandisa herself has named her son. They insist on giving him a new name, too. Mandisa is horrified by the thought, but again has to abide by their wish. They call her son *Mxolisi* and have him baptized a few weeks later.

Mandisa has to do most of the household chores. She is the first to get up in the morning to prepare coffee and breakfast, and make sure all the children in the household get ready for school. China gets a job as a labourer, which he does not like. He tells Mandisa he hates his job and that Mandisa could have had an abortion so he could have continued his education. This reminds Mandisa of Ribba, the girl that died during an illegal abortion.

Mandisa asks for permission to resume her education, but her wish is not granted and the decision postponed.

Suddenly, Mandisa finds that China has left. She tells the reader she has not heard from him in nearly twenty years. Mandisa decides to leave, too, and looks to rent a *hokkie* of her own. Luckily for Mxolisi, there are two older boys at the main house who look after him a lot and take him along on their adventures. However, tragedy unfolds when one day there is a police raid and Zazi and Mzamo, the two older boys, hide in a wardrobe. Mxolisi, too young to understand the situation (he is only four years old), tells the police where they are. He has to watch how the two boys are shot by the police when they try to escape.

As a result of the incident, Mxolisi is mute for a prolonged period of time. After some months, he is taken to a *sangoma*, a soothsayer, who tries to explain to Mandisa that she has to stop resenting Mxolisi.
Meanwhile Nono and Khaya get married. Additionally, at the wedding, Mandisa meets Lungile. They become intimate. Mandisa is pregnant again and gives birth to Lunga.

Almost two years after Mxolisi last uttered a word, he finally asks about his father. Unfortunately, Mandisa still has no idea as to his whereabouts. To Mandisa's surprise, Mxolisi has never asked where Zazi and Mzamo are. This worries her, but first and foremost, she is happy that Mxolisi speaks again.

A couple of months later, Lungile leaves to train as a freedom fighter. As a result, Mandisa has to look after the two children by herself. Only later does she find out that Mxolisi has not attended school for a very long time. She persuades him to return, only to discover that he has become involved in politics. At the same time, wherever she goes, people she hardly knows tell her that Mxolisi has a very good reputation in the neighbourhood. People tell her that he even saved a girl from being raped by a group of men.

The chapter closes saying that the same people who lauded her and Mxolisi now despise her for being the mother of a murderer.

Important quotations explained

> 'Can you imagine that all these cattle belong to one Boer? We have been driving, for over an hour, through ONE farm?'

This statement is given by the driver who drives Mandisa and her mother back home to Cape Town. It is significant for two reasons: Firstly, it implies that the black majority is poor and finds it hard to imagine that a single individual would own as much land as this farmer. Secondly, referring to the Boers, the driver is alluding to both Dutch and British imperialism in South Africa. In both Afrikaans and Dutch, *Boer* is the word for *farmer*. In South Africa, the word *Boer* refers to settlers of Dutch origin who migrated to South Africa from the 18th century onwards. For an extensive period of time, the area had been controlled by the Dutch East India Company, before the British annexed the territory. Thus, the driver criticizes the colonization of South Africa and the taking of land from indigenous people. This nicely ties in with the next quote:

> 'Stole them from us. STOLE everything from us'

The driver explains that when the *Boers* (Dutch settlers) arrived in the country, they did not possess any cattle or other animals whatsoever. Therefore, they *stole* them from others. Furthermore, the driver here employs language typical of post-colonial literature: *Us* and *them* are polar opposites. He emphasizes that *they* (the Boers) and the driver are not members of the same community (the use of polar opposites is called a *binary opposition*). It can be inferred that South

Africa is a divided country.

> 'This has happened to him as much as it has happened to me', I said.

By *this* Mandisa is referring to her pregnancy. She says that she and China are equally responsible so, naturally, he should be told about Mandisa's expecting a baby. This stands in stark contrast to her mother, who maintains that Mandisa is solely responsible and that the pregnancy is her fault.

> 'The teachers have helped me get a scholarship. They think I am bright, I deserve to get a higher education. And Father has been wonderfully cooperative ... I have his complete support.'

This passage is important with regard to gender roles in South African society. In the previous chapter we learn that Mandisa has been doing even better at school. It does not occur to China that Mandisa would like to continue her own education. China is rather self-centred here in saying that he is the one who deserves the scholarship. In the ensuing paragraph we learn that this upsets Mandisa very much. Also, as the chapter unfolds, it turns out that China's father is not at all "cooperative" when it comes to Mandisa's education. Mandisa is thus discriminated against in two different ways: as a woman her position within the black community is inferior to men and as a black her position is inferior to whites.

> He was a white man and a priest.

The discrimination against Mandisa becomes apparent if we compare it with the authority of the priest. Not only is he a priest, but he is also a man and white. This gives whatever he says significantly more authority.

> Joy, pure and simple ... I think that comes closest to describing what I felt.

After her son is born, Mandisa's feelings towards him are ambiguous. In the paragraph preceding this quote, she says that the words "forgive", "accept", and "welcome" are not exactly the right words to aptly describe her feelings. And even the phrase "pure joy" is immediately qualified by saying that Mandisa "thinks" it comes "closest" to what her real feelings are. Her feelings towards her son turn out to play a crucial role later in the chapter.

> '... we live our lives through advice, consultation and allowing or bowing down to the voice of the majority. Never can I trust my eye above the eyes of the many, who are my family, my clan.'

While women have to obey men in South African society, men are bound by the decisions of the *clan*, i.e. the extended family. This becomes most important when the two families negotiate the implications of Mandisa's pregnancy. Note, however, how none of the major characters in the novel are able to make decisions independently.

> Were it not for him, of course, I would still be in school. Instead, I was forced into being a wife, forever abandoning my dreams, hopes, aspirations. For ever.

Here it becomes obvious why her son is such a burden for Mandisa. Not only does she have to look after the baby, motherhood also inevitably means marriage in South African society, which is why she is forced into marrying China and living with his family. This means that all of her previous hopes and ambitions are shattered.

> 'What, exactly, has happened to that dog?' Mama spat out. (p.119)

> 'Is that not tying oneself to a dog in a patch of nettles?' (p.130)

> The dog in the patch of nettles. The dog and I. So soon, though? So soon, he had started feeling his life a waste ... something he would always resent?

Mandisa's mother liberally resorts to the term "dog" to refer to people she despises. For Mandisa, this is more unusual and it shows that Mandisa, too, starts to dehumanize people in calling them the names of animals. A "dog in a patch of nettles" also implies that China's reactions would be predetermined and that he could not possibly reflect on the situation and act differently. Having had to take up a job as a labourer and not being able to resume his education, China's feelings turn bitter.

> These children went around the township screaming at the top of their voices: LIBERATION NOW, EDUCATION LATER! and ONE SETTLER, ONE BULLET!

Mxolisi's return to school also entails his becoming interested in politics. During the freedom movement of the 1980s, the slogan *One Settler, One Bullet* was a rallying cry encouraging indigenous people to kill white settlers who support the apartheid regime. Some even interpreted the slogan in a way that would mean to kill all white people in South Africa. The term was a response to the governments slogan *One Man, One Vote* and can be said to have played a role in the killing of Amy Biehl.
In the novel, the slogan obviously exerts a significant influence on Mxolisi. Mandisa makes it clear that taking part in the liberation movement also means that education plays only a secondary role, if any at all. In contrast to Mandisa, Mxolisi is not a good student and does not even finish primary school.

Chapter 9 6am - Thursday 26 August

Summary

The police have just left the house and Mandisa and Dwadwa look after the children: Lunga is badly hurt; he has several bruises and a cut lip, but no bones are broken. Siziwe is in complete shock. She finally tells Mandisa that Mxolisi had been in the house earlier, possibly to hide something, and then left again very quickly. Furthermore, Mandisa senses that there is something else that Siziwe tries to tell her. However, it seems too horrible to say and Mandisa lets her be.
Two of their neighbours come round, but before they can talk about what people on the street are saying Dwadwa sends them away. Lunga says he wants to go to school the next morning and Dwadwa wants to go to work. Mandisa is going to stay home in case Mxolisi comes back.
Toward the end of the chapter, Dwadwa says that he anticipated the fact that Mxolisi would bring great shame and trouble on the family one day.

Important quotations explained

> Or what I feared, and refused to accept, she had been trying to tell me.

Mandisa here, of course, is talking about the murder. She does not want to admit to herself that Mxolisi might be the murderer.

> And he isn't going to come back here ... wherever he is, he must know, by now, that they are looking for him.

In this foreshadowing, Dwadwa suggests that Mxolisi might not come back. For now, it is unclear whether that pertains only to the time that the police are searching for him or to an extended period of time.

Chapter 10

Summary

The first part of chapter 10 relates Mandisa's memories of what her grandfather tells her when she is a child. While Mandisa's grandfather Tatomkhulu says that it was the explorer Vasco da Gama who named the Cape "Cape of Storm", he maintains that the storms in people's hearts are more significant. He tells Mandisa about an event that took place in 1857, in which the Xhosa nation killed all its cattle and burned its fields, as a prophecy had promised this would drive out the white oppressors. When, in the aftermath of the event, people had no food and were faced with starvation, the colonizers, under Sir George Grey, offered the Xhosa labour contracts that would grant payment, but would also make the Xhosa dependent on white settlers.

Important Quotations explained

> 'Those dogs I work for!'
>
> 'We have come thus to hunger, for white people stole our land.'

Both these quotations are taken from the beginning of the chapter when Mandisa's parents complain about their white employers. We can see here that the labelling of human beings as animals, and as dogs in particular, can be found throughout the book covering all the generations that Mandisa talks about, including her own. The quotations also demonstrate what Tatomkhulu, Mandisa's grandfather, talks about later on in the chapter:

> 'Did he [Vasco da Gama] not know that the biggest storm was the storm they themselves brought?

Tatomkhulu says that the roots of people's hatred is inherent in South African society and dates back several generations. The past and present actions of whites are responsible for the suffering of the Xhosa and of blacks in general in South Africa. Tatomkhulu also makes a biblical reference when he refers to the storm (cf. Hosea 8:7 "He who sows the wind shall reap the whirlwind." - See also in chapter 10 of the novel: "The hatred has but multiplied.").

> First, we keep cattle for a man to offer *lobola* to his in-laws [...]

Mandisa has just asked her grandfather why people keep cattle at all. Her grandfather gives several reasons, none of which is convincing. This passage can be read as an ironic criticism of South African society, in which old customs and traditions are more important than their actual usefulness.

> 'Have your teachers told you anything about Nongqawuse?'

According to the legend, Nongquawuse was one of two girls who said they had met three spirits in the fields. Nongquawuse said that the spirits advise the people to kill all cattle and destroy all crops, which would then usher in a new era of history, in which whites would be expelled from the country. To the present day, it remains unclear who the instigator of the prophecies actually was. The Xhosa had been fighting against colonization for many years, but the depopulation that took place in the aftermath of the cattle-killing encouraged even more Europeans to move to South Africa.

> Sir George Grey leading the pack. They came. Bringing gifts of food to the starving, dying people. Bringing a golden opportunity never to starve again.

Sir George Grey became governor of the Cape Colony in 1854. He played a key role in establishing British authority in South Africa, as well as having a missionary agenda. Tatomkhulu specifically mentions the enticement of working in the mines and the opportunity to "get paid money".

> 'At Isandlwana, with spear and shield, Cetywayo's impis defeated the might British army and its guns.'

The Battle of Isandlwana (in 1879), took place when the British tried to invade the Zulu Kingdom. The battle was indeed won by the poorly equipped Zulus. However, this caused the British to adopt a far more destructive approach in a second invasion of the Zulu Kingdom. Mandisa's grandfather rightly points out that the anti-colonial efforts turned out to be "All to no avail". N.B.: The term *impi* is a Zulu expression denoting a regiment (a large group of armed men).

1pm - Thursday 26 August

Summary

At one o'clock, Mandisa wakes up. Siziwe tells her that Lunga has been picked up by some boys in a car. Siziwe says that this might be linked with the incident involving the white girl.

After Mandisa and Siziwe have had something to eat, Reverend Mananga visits the house. As he expects the police to be eavesdropping, he writes a note telling Mandisa to take the taxi (i.e. bus) and get off at the last stop. On the bus, a girl hands her a note (in hand-writing that Mandisa recognizes to be Mananga's) telling her to get off one stop after her. Having done that, Mandisa is driven to a house where Mananga has arranged for her to meet her son Mxolisi.

Mxolisi tells her what has happened and that everybody, including the police, holds him responsible for the killing. He first denies having killed the girl; it turns out that he was one out of many involved in the killing. Both Mandisa and Mxolisi weep and hug each other.

Important Quotations explained

> 'The one who was killed?' I couldn't believe I'd asked that. Why was that the first thing that came to my mind, I wondered. When had I started thinking Mxolisi's absence might be linked to those troubles?

This statement must be seen as ironic and the question as rhetorical, although Mandisa has been hesitant to admit that she thinks Mxolisi is involved in the murder. While in the previous paragraph she addresses the girl's mother directly ("your daughter"), it becomes clear that, while the girl's mother has to accept the death of her child, Mandisa has to accept Mxolisi's involvement in the murder.

> 'Mama, believe me, I was just one of a hundred people who threw stones at her car.' '. . . many people stabbed her.'

The fact that it might be impossible to ascertain who did what exactly in the assault on the car and the subsequent murder of the white girl, might in itself be meaningful: It could have been Mxolisi or any other person present during the attack. Mxolisi is representative of young men in Guguletu, his life and background as it is described by Mandisa could be any other's in the township. Mxolisi stands for his generation as a whole.

Chapter 11

Summary

Chapter 11 is framed by direct appeals to the student's mother. In this chapter, Mandisa ponders the implications of the murder: She talks about shame and anger, about the question of guilt, and the different ways in which the two mothers mourn.

Important Quotations explained

> But now, my Sister-Mother, do I help him hide?

Mandisa addresses the student's mother as her "Sister-Mother" (capital letters). She does this twice in this chapter. Not only are they both mothers, they both have to deal with what has happened in their own ways. Furthermore, calling her "Sister-Mother", Mandisa reaches out to her and creates a bond between the two mothers. In addition, asking a rhetorical question, Mandisa enters a dialogue both with her counterpart and with the reader. (She does this a lot in this chapter.)

> Shame and anger fill me day and night. Shame at what my son has done. Anger at what has been done to him.

Mandisa implies here that her son is both perpetrator and victim alike. Note how Mandisa uses the passive voice ("has been done") to emphasize that Mxolisi is also a victim. There are people and forces whose actions are directed at (and against) Mxolisi.

> And the police. How can they tell, with absolute certainty, which of those knives that rained on your poor child killed her?

This nicely ties in with the last quotation in the previous chapter. Apart from the fact that Mxolisi is an archetype representing his generation, one could also argue that Mandisa tries to downplay Mxolisi's role in the attack.

Guguletu, much later

Summary

Skonana and Qwati, Mandisa's neighbours, along with Lindiwe and Yolisa, who live in the same street, visit Mandisa to share her grief. Mandisa feels that her neighbours give her strength. While many people despise her for what her son has done, Mandisa is relieved to learn that there are people who are there for her.
The chapter closes with Mandisa comparing the losses the two mothers have to deal with. She claims that her loss is shameful, while her sister-mother's is glorious.

Important Quotations explained

> I know there are some among my friends and neighbours who feel for me - who understand my pain.

While Mxolisi is accused of murder, it is his mother who is in pain. It consoles Mandisa that there are people who actually understand her. By and large, the novel as a whole can be read as Mandisa's attempt to cope with her son being a murderer. It is thus as much about Mandisa as it is about Mxolisi. Note that whilst Mxolisi, the aggressor, is male, the student, her mother, Mandisa and her neighbours who come to console, are all female.

> Irretrievable loss. Be consoled, however. Be consoled, for with your loss comes no shame. No deep sense of personal failure. Only glory.

Mandisa implies that she suffers more than her sister-mother because of the public disgrace that her son's murder entails. The phrase "personal failure" means that Mandisa thinks she has failed as a mother which is also what Dwadwa implies just before the police raid.
In contrast to Mandisa's shame, the student's death means glory for her mother: The girl is made into a martyr, a heroic character who was killed despite her noble intentions. (Mandisa goes on to encourage her to use this as a source of strength.)

Chapter 12

Summary

At the beginning of chapter 12, Mandisa addresses Mxolisi's future prospects had he not become a murderer. Mandisa explains that, just like his father, Mxolisi has had no chance of improving his overall situation. She asserts there is no hope for Mxolisi, and in fact for his whole generation.

Important Quotations explained

> His tomorrows were his yesterday. Nothing. [....] A glaring void.

By "tomorrows" Mandisa means his future; by "yesterday" she means his past. In saying that both his past and his future is "a glaring void", Mandisa tries to say that Mxolisi's outlook is hopeless.

> He had already seen his tomorrows; in the defeated stoop of his father's shoulders.

This quote is an interesting one: Who does Mandisa refer to when she speaks of Mxolisi's father? Obviously, his real (i.e. biological) father has never returned. Could she be talking about Dwadwa, who Mxolisi insists is not his real father? Anyway, Mandisa's point here is that, if anything, Mxolisi can expect to have a job as a labourer just like his "father", Dwadwa.

> Such stark sign-posts to his tomorrow. Hope still-born in his heart. [....] the lost generation.

By "sign-posts" Mandisa means her son's expectations as to how his life would probably unfold. Therefore, hope is still-born, i.e. born dead. Finally, Mandisa argues that this is true not only for Mxolisi as an individual, but for his generation as a whole.

Guguletu, late afternoon, Wednesday 25 August

Summary

The final pages of the novel describe, in great detail, the attack on the car, which culminates in murder: At first, the yellow car is just one out of many in Guguletu. Then, people realize there is a white person in the car. First, the car is rocked (shaken), and subsequently stoned. The five students leave the car and try to make it to a nearby garage. The mob chases them. Some have knives. The students plead with the mob, but to no avail. The crowd has been chanting "one settler, one bullet". The white student is killed mercilessly.

Important Quotations Explained

> The pack races towards the source of the cry, as one, echoing: 'One settler, one bullet.'

The term *pack* is zoological and would most typically refer to *a pack of wolves* or *a pack of hounds*, for example. It is striking how the presence of a white person unifies the black youngsters. The constant repetition of the phrase "One settler, one bullet" underlines the inevitability of the outcome.

> The mob, like hounds, give chase, yelling and screaming in glee. [....] BOERS, THEY ARE DOGS!

The mob is here explicitly referred to as "hounds" (i.e. dogs used for hunting). Likewise, the crowd refers to Boers, i.e. white settlers, as dogs. This dehumanizes both groups. It lets the murder appear less barbaric as it is more natural for animals to kill, especially for hounds. Boers are referred to as "dogs": For the mob, it feels just to kill whites; and it is not necessarily illegal to kill an animal. Dehumanizing "Boers" enables the mob to justify murder.

> We had been cheering him on since the day he was born. Before he was born. Long before.

Blacks have been holding whites responsible as a group rather than as individuals. Thus, Mandisa argues that in making whites responsible as a race, people have actually encouraged Mxolisi to commit murder and to hold an individual responsible for the deeds of others. Ironically, the victim wanted to help the black community.

> The enactment of the deep, dark, private yearnings of a subjugated race. The consummation of inevitable senseless catastrophe.

This quotation takes up two ideas we have already seen in previous examples: Firstly, Mxolisi acts on behalf of his race as a whole (*subjugated* means "defeated and controlled"). Secondly, Mandisa says that catastrophe is inevitable, i.e. it cannot be avoided. It makes sense for her to bring this point up on the last page of the novel as this is what she set out to do at the very beginning: She wants to make people understand why the murder was committed and that the "wrath of his [Mxolisi's] race" played a pivotal role in the killing and made Mxolisi only an "agent". This idea ties in nicely with Mandisa's final thought: Even if Mxolisi had not become a murderer on that particular day, it is likely he would have become one eventually.

6 Literary Devices Used in 'Mother to Mother'

alliteration repetition of the same sound at the beginning of a word
Example: "rude reality" (chapter 4)

allusion a brief, often implicit reference to a person, event, place, phrase, etc.
Example: Shaka, a Zulu king, is said to have been conceived during what began as a sort of sexual foreplay without penetration. Mandisa alludes to this when she describes the "play sex" she and China have resulting in Mxolisi's conception (chapter 7).

anaphora the repetition of the same word or phrase at the beginning of several consecutive sentences (or clauses)
Example: In Chapter 6, Mandisa describes how the police search the house: "They looked", "They pulled", "They knocked", "They tore", "they simply dismantled" etc. The repetition of the word "they" also serves to emphasize the respective verbs.

binary opposition a pair of terms that are diametrically opposed
Examples: us - them, children - adults, blacks - whites, individual - clan, women - men, honour - shame (Mandisa aptly demonstrates how people think in terms of polar opposites.)

comparison comparing two or more things to show similarities or contrasts
Example: When Mandisa compares her own childhood with Mxolisi's, she says that "Guns are *as common as*

marbles were when we were growing up." (emphasis added)

dramatic irony when the reader knows something that the characters do not

Examples: There are two examples in chapter 3: Firstly, Mandisa worries about her daughter, while it is Mxolisi who she should be worried about. Secondly, people in Blouvlei cannot believe rumours of the removal and dismiss it as unthinkable.

euphemism a figure of speech in which a harsh or blunt expression is avoided and a milder one is used instead

Examples: In a simile in chapter 5, Mandisa speaks of "unruly children destroying a colony of anthills" when she refers to the destruction of tin shacks by white men. Furthermore, her reference to human beings as "dogs" is euphemistic, as is the expression *necklacing*.

flashback interruption to show an event that takes place earlier in time to help the reader understand better

Examples: Mandisa uses flashbacks to shed light on her own childhood and on how life has been changing over the course of South African history.

foreshadowing subtle hints at how the novel will unfold

Example: In chapter 2, Mandisa speaks of "A day that spells closure. Heavy as a prison door." The imagery used in this chapter foreshadows the police hunt for Mxolisi and the events that follow. (Other examples from chapter 2 include: "gun-metal grey", "fiercely intimate flames", "fists stabbing air", "unsmiling heavens".)

imagery language relating to one or all of the five senses

Example: Look at how Mandisa makes the reader hear, feel, and see the removal from Blouvlei and people's new homes in Guguletu (chapter 5).

inversion changing the normal word order in a sentence

Example: "With impunity they killed our people in the past." (Mandisa talking about the police in chapter 4)

juxtaposition placing two things side by side in order to

compare them
Example: In chapter 5, Mandisa juxtaposes living in Blouvlei and in Guguletu.

metaphor the comparison of two unlike things, *not* using the words "as" or "like"
Example: "Whites are dogs." (Chapter 5)

motif a recurrent idea, a dominant element in a literary text that can be used to interpret a theme
Examples: dogs (dehumanization), light and darkness, silence,

personification the attribution of human qualities, powers, and feelings to abstractions or objects
Example: "However, each time the same *stubborn silence greeted* my investigation" (chapter 5, emphasis added)

repetition the repetition of sounds, syllables, words, phrases, etc. for effect
Examples: the word "chance" at the beginning of chapter 12; the phrase "every day" in chapter 4 when Guguletu is described as a violent place; the word "pandemonium" in chapter 3

rhetorical question a question that does not require an answer or a question to which an answer is immediately supplied; a powerful statement put as a question
Example: In Chapter 1 Mandisa uses rhetorical questions extensively to structure the text.

simile the comparison of two unlike things, using the words "as" or "like"
Example: "Died like dogs." (Chapter 8) Mandisa uses this simile to describe how Mzamo and Zazi are killed by the police.

symbol anything that represents or stands for something else
Example: 12 (the number of chapters in the novel) stands for what is complete or forms a whole. Furthermore, in the US, 12 people are appointed to sit on a jury in court, so the 12 chapters might stand for the

jury judging Mxolisi.

theme a central, abstract concept explored in a work of literature

Examples: motherhood, guilt, shame, discrimination,

7 A Very Brief History of South Africa

1487-1488 The first European navigator reached South Africa. (Europe's prime concern was finding a sea-route to India. This was achieved by Vasco da Gama in his voyage from 1497 to 1499.)

1652 A Dutch colony was established (Cape Colony) by the *Dutch East India Company*. At first, the colony was meant for re-supply with regard to trade with Asia, but it soon also became a settler colony. The settlers were known as *Boers* (the Durch word for *farmers*).

1806 The British founded a colony, i.e. they took the colony from the Dutch. Some Boers moved northwards (encountering the Xhosa), which later led to the formation of the Orange Free State and the Republic of Transvaal. After founding the colony, the British began conquering more and more territories in South Africa. The British East India company, too, was first interested in securing trade routes with Asia, but soon also focussed on territorial expansion.

1856-1857 A Xhosa teenager prophesied that the Xhosa should kill all their cattle and crops. Nongqawuse, the prophetess, argued that this would make the whites leave the country. It did not work, but rather precipitated white domination in South Africa. As a result of the cattle-killing, many blacks accepted labour contracts with the whites. (Basically, the cattle-killing was national suicide for the Xhosa.)

1879 During the Battle of Isandlwana, the Zulu Kingdom defeated a whole British regiment despite having inferior weapons. (The Zulus had been the dominant tribe in South Africa before the British arrived.)

1880s Gold and diamonds were found in South Africa, including the Boer settlement. This is why the British later sought a pretext for war. The Gold Rush started. Indian labourers were brought to work in mines and sugar farms.

1899-1902 The Dutch had declined joining a federation with the British. During the Anglo-Boer War, the Dutch states of *Transvaal* and the *Orange Free State* were defeated by the British and became part of the British Empire.

1910 The *Union of South Africa*, a so-called *dominion* of the British crown, was formed. It was governed by whites. (Blacks, throughout the world, had no political rights.)

1912 ANC (African National Congress) was founded.

1948 Policy of apartheid was introduced banning blacks from owning land (outside certain areas) and depriving blacks from access to proper education and health services.

1953 Bantu Education Act: Schools were entirely controlled by the state and racially separate. Spending on the education of blacks was minimal; blacks should only be taught to know what they needed to become unskilled labourers.

1960 South Africa became a republic, i.e. independent. The ANC was banned and its leaders (Nelson Mandela and others) were sent to prison.

1962 Sabotage Act: The definition of sabotage was extended to include strikes and anti-government publications. The accused were thought of as guilty until proven otherwise.

1970s Blacks were forcefully resettled to so-called "homelands" (About three million people were displaced). International sanctions ensued.

1970s and 80s Revolts against the apartheid regime increased and became more violent. It was during this time that the rallying cry "one settler, one bullet" came up, parodying the slogan "one man, one vote".

1989 De Klerk, the new President of South Africa, initialized racial reconciliation: Apartheid laws were repealed. The country, however, saw another outbreak of violence from radical groups. The African National Congress announced an operation called *Operation Barcelona*, condoning violence in support of striking teachers (cf. chapters 2,3, and 12 in the novel). (August 25, 1993: Amy Biehl, a white American scholar and anti-apartheid activist was murdered.)

1994 First democratic elections were held in South Africa. Nelson Mandela became President.

20425323R00041

Printed in Poland
by Amazon Fulfillment
Poland Sp. z o.o., Wrocław